ENGLAND
BEFORE
1485

ISLE OF MAN

SAINT GEORGE

George was a Roman soldier who was born in Palestine about 280AD. In legend he's famous for killing the dragon. He never came near England so it's a bit of a mystery why his red cross became the national flag.

ANGLESEY
Druid HQ

OFFA'S DYKE

CAENARFON CASTLE
where Edward I made
his son Prince of Wales

WALES

CHEDDAR
GORGE

GLASTONBURY

ALBION
is an ancient name for
England. It means white.
Perhaps the name came
from the White Cliffs.

TINTAGEL
which some say was
King Arthur's Camelot

SOMERSET LEVELS
where Alfred hid

NEW FOREST
where William
Rufus was killed

SALCOMBE
3,000 year old
shipwrecks found

LANDS
END

NEWCASTLE

NORTH SEA

JARROW
where Bede
wrote his history

HADRIAN'S WALL

YORK
here Constantine
the Great was
declared Roman
mperor in 306AD

LANCASTER

1st ENGLISH
HOUSE
Star Carr 9000BC

VIKING LONGBOAT

BATTLE OF
BOSWORTH FIELD 1485

SHERWOOD
FOREST

THE WASH
where King John was
said to have lost his
treasure in 1216

EAST
ANGLIA

HAPPISBURGH
1st human footprints
900,000BC

OXFORD
UNIVERSITY
founded
c1096

CAMBRIDGE

ELY
Hereward's
HQ

SUTTON
HOO

STONEHENGE

Temple of Claudius
COLCHESTER

THE WHITE TOWER

THANET
where
Hengist and
Horsa
landed

RUNNYMEDE
where John signed
Magna Carta

VINCHESTER
Alfred the
Great's capital

NORMAN SHIP

CANTERBURY
CATHEDRAL

BATTLE OF
HASTINGS

DEAL
where
Julius
Caesar
landed

SLE OF
VIGHT

WHITE CLIFFS

CALAIS

THE STORY OF ENGLAND

ORION CHILDREN'S BOOKS

First published in Great Britain in 2015
by Orion Children's Books
This edition published in 2016 by
Hodder and Stoughton

1 3 5 7 9 10 8 6 4 2

A CIP catalogue record for this book
is available from the British Library.

ISBN 978 1 4440 1495 2

Printed and bound in China

The paper and board used in this book are from well-managed forests
and other responsible sources.

Orion Children's Books
An imprint of
Hachette Children's Group
Part of Hodder and Stoughton
Carmelite House
50 Victoria Embankment
London EC4Y 0DZ

An Hachette UK Company
www.hachette.co.uk

www.hachettechildrens.co.uk

THE
STORY
OF
ENGLAND

RICHARD BRASSEY

Orion
Children's Books

THE STORY OF ENGLAND

The footprints of the very first English people we know about were found in the mud on a beach in Norfolk. They arrived nearly a million years ago. They weren't quite the same as we are. They had smaller brains, lower foreheads and bigger chins. And of course England wouldn't be called England until much later. There were no beaches in Norfolk then. The British Isles were connected to the rest of Europe by dry land.

12,000 BC

It was at the end of the last Ice Age that modern humans like us began arriving in England across the plain of Doggerland which now lies at the bottom of the North Sea. Perhaps they made their way up the Thames, then a tributary of the river Rhine.

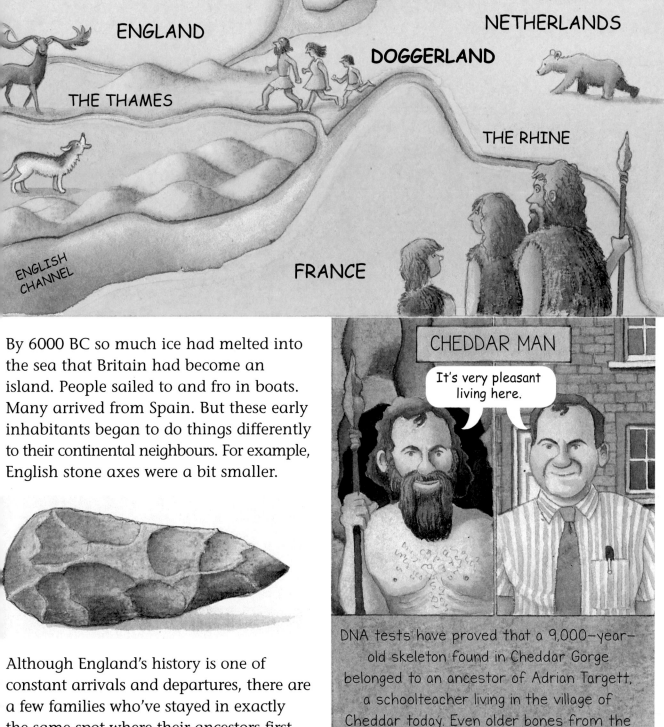

DOGGER HILLS

ENGLAND

NETHERLANDS

DOGGERLAND

THE THAMES

THE RHINE

ENGLISH CHANNEL

FRANCE

By 6000 BC so much ice had melted into the sea that Britain had become an island. People sailed to and fro in boats. Many arrived from Spain. But these early inhabitants began to do things differently to their continental neighbours. For example, English stone axes were a bit smaller.

Although England's history is one of constant arrivals and departures, there are a few families who've stayed in exactly the same spot where their ancestors first settled thousands of years ago.

CHEDDAR MAN

It's very pleasant living here.

DNA tests have proved that a 9,000-year-old skeleton found in Cheddar Gorge belonged to an ancestor of Adrian Targett, a schoolteacher living in the village of Cheddar today. Even older bones from the same cave suggest that some of our ancestors may have been cannibals!

9

STONEHENGE (3000-2000 BC)

Stonehenge is the most famous ancient monument in England but similar stone circles were built all over western Europe during this period. We don't really know their purpose. They were probably places of worship. By this time much of England had been cleared of woods and tracks criss-crossed the land. Modern roads often still follow their courses today.

Farmers grew wheat and barley and kept pigs and cattle. Sheep arrived during this period and must have been brought over in boats. In fact, lots of trade took place with the rest of Europe. The wrecks of several ships have been found from this time with their cargoes still on board.

Baa! Baaa!

In 325 BC an Ancient Greek merchant, Pytheas, visited. He was the first known person ever to write about England. He described many small kingdoms living peacefully together in what he called Bretannike, from which we get the name Britain.

What's for dinner?

Nettle gruel

The natives live in thatched cottages, have simple manners and are happy with plain food.

In 55 BC the famous Roman general, Julius Caesar, who'd been busy conquering Gaul (modern day France) reached the English Channel and thought he'd sail over for a look. The following year he popped over again with a bigger army, marching as far north as the Thames before returning to France. He kept a diary of everything he saw.

Ninety years later, the Romans invaded properly. In the meantime the people of southern England had decided they liked the Roman way of doing things. They started building Roman-style square houses and importing Roman luxuries like wine and glass.

All the same they weren't too happy when the legions arrived in 43 AD. There was a big battle in Kent which the Romans won. As soon as it was safe, Emperor Claudius sailed over with 28 elephants and marched into the ancient tribal capital of Colchester. They called their new colony Britannia.

BOUDICA GOAD

The Romans had only been in England for 20 years when Boudica, a tribal queen, united the native people in revolt. She burnt down Colchester, London and St Albans before being defeated. Nobody is sure where or how she died.

11

HADRIAN'S WALL (completed 128 AD)

Hadrian's wall marked the northern boundary of the Roman Empire. It was 73 miles long and was probably plastered smooth and painted white which must have astonished the Pictish tribes to the north. The border between England and Scotland is almost the same today.

Blimey! What is it?

Search me.

Thousands of Roman officials, merchants and troops settled in Britannia during the 350 years it was a Roman colony. When they retired Roman soldiers were encouraged to stay and given land to farm. They introduced new fruits and vegetables such as cherries, figs, turnips, cabbages and peas. The remains of prosperous Roman farmhouses have been found all over southern England.

DRUIDS

The Romans were fascinated by these native priests and their rituals involving mistletoe and white bulls. Julius Caesar wrote that they made human sacrifices. Others wrote that they practised magic. But the Druids were so secretive that the Romans didn't really know much about them at all.

LONDINIUM

Founded to guard the Roman bridge across the Thames, London soon grew into a busy port. After Boudica's revolt it became the capital, with many fine buildings, its own colosseum and a massive wall (a few bits of which can still be seen today).

Although England prospered under the Romans, it was not always peaceful. There were frequent civil wars and at least one plague which killed many people. In the late 4th century Rome itself faced invasion by German tribes. The legions left for the Continent and by 410 AD the Roman government in England had collapsed.

KING ARTHUR

OLD KING COLE

Where are my pipe and fiddlers?

Just two of the kings said to have ruled in England after the Romans. They may have been real people but the stories about them were made up later.

Can you help us?

Nice here isn't it, Hengist?

Not much is known about the time immediately after the Romans left. It is said that in 449 AD a king named Vortigern asked two Anglo-Saxon brothers, Hengist and Horsa, to sail over from northern Germany to help him fight off Pictish invaders from Scotland. They settled in Kent and liked it so much that they refused to leave after the job was done. Instead they invited hundreds of their relatives to join them and soon moved into East Anglia as well.

Nobody is certain how many Anglo-Saxons arrived but by 600 AD they had settled and ruled most of what we now call England. Some counties are still called by the names of their kingdoms.

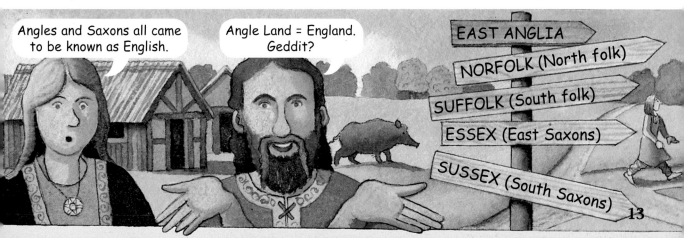

Angles and Saxons all came to be known as English.

Angle Land = England. Geddit?

EAST ANGLIA

NORFOLK (North folk)

SUFFOLK (South folk)

ESSEX (East Saxons)

SUSSEX (South Saxons)

SUTTON HOO

In 1939 the remains of a ship were found beneath one of 17 burial mounds at Sutton Hoo in Suffolk. Within it were the famous helmet, swords, jewellery and other treasure now in the British Museum. It's thought to have contained the body of Rœdwald, a 7th century Saxon king of East Anglia.

Many native Britons had converted to Christianity during Roman times but the new arrivals worshipped pagan gods, whose names – Tiw, Woden, Thor and Freya – we still use in our days of the week: Tuesday, Wednesday, Thursday and Friday.

Missionaries soon arrived from Rome and Ireland to convert them to Christianity. By the end of the 7th century most Anglo Saxons had accepted the church of Rome.

ST AUGUSTINE

Can we still use our old days of the week?

Sent by the Pope to convert Æthelberht, King of Kent, to Christianity, he became the first Archbishop of Canterbury in 597 AD.

HOW WE KNOW ABOUT EARLY ENGLISH HISTORY

Roman historians had not been very interested in far-off Britannia. The Anglo-Saxons were the first to really write down all the important things that happened.

BEDE (673–735 AD)

known as 'the Father of English History' because of his history of the early church.

THE ANGLO SAXON CHRONICLE

was begun in King Alfred's reign and kept up to date until the Norman Conquest. Although not always reliable, it is packed with information about those times.

OFFA'S DYKE

Named after Offa, an 8th century Saxon King of Mercia, this may have been dug to keep the Welsh out. It roughly follows today's border between England and Wales.

THE VIKINGS

Big changes were happening in Europe which caused many Norwegians and Danes, known as Vikings, to cross the North Sea in their famous longships and invade England. Viking *berserks*, who charged howling into battle wearing wolfskins, terrified the English. "Never before has such terror appeared in Britain," wrote one English scholar. By 870 AD thousands of Vikings had settled in eastern England.

ALFRED THE GREAT (849-899) – KING OF THE ANGLO SAXONS

As a boy Alfred met the Pope in Rome.

You'll have to help with housework!

After he became King of Wessex, the Vikings attacked and chased him into the Somerset marshes where legend says he hid in a peasant woman's cottage . . .

How can I save my kingdom?

My cakes!

Left to watch her cakes he let them burn. His mind was on more important things.

Finally he beat the Vikings who agreed to stay only in the East of England.

After defeating the Vikings, Alfred started many institutions we still know today. He founded many fortified towns or *burhs* which we call 'boroughs'. He reformed the legal and tax systems, encouraged education in English instead of Latin and built new ships for the navy. His daughter, Æthelflæd, continued to push back the Vikings. His grandson, Æthelstan, completed the job to become the first King of all England.

Gradually the Anglo-Saxons and Vikings mixed together. Harold is sometimes known as the 'last English (as in Anglo-Saxon) King', although he was half Viking. Nine months after he came to the throne William the Conqueror and his Normans invaded.

THE BATTLE OF HASTINGS 1066

Isn't that Harold?

King Harold died in the battle which the Normans won, although historians can't agree if it's Harold shown with an arrow in his eye in the famous Bayeux Tapestry.

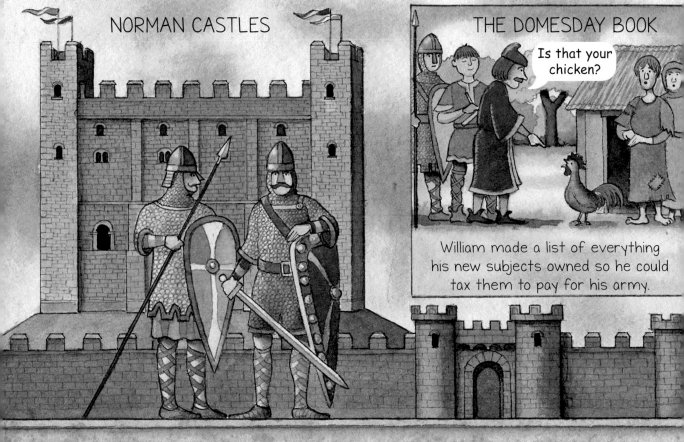

NORMAN CASTLES

THE DOMESDAY BOOK

Is that your chicken?

William made a list of everything his new subjects owned so he could tax them to pay for his army.

There weren't many Normans. They built strong castles from which to lord it over the English. The White Tower in the Tower of London is the most famous one left.

William the Conqueror and his Normans were just another lot of Vikings who had previously settled in northern France. He spent much of his time in France where he was finally buried in 1087.

The Conqueror left Normandy to his oldest son Robert, and England to his second son, William. William, called Rufus because of his red face and beard, had hardly ever visited England before. When he was killed, his younger brother, Henry, took over and promptly pinched his oldest brother's crown as well, reuniting England and Normandy.

WILLIAM RUFUS

Rufus was shot dead by a friend while hunting in the New Forest. Nobody is sure if it was an accident or not.

HEREWARD THE WAKE

Saxon Hereward led a revolt against the Normans but was defeated when they were tipped off about a secret path through the marshes to his Ely HQ.

The Norman barons and knights spoke a type of French and thought of themselves as superior to the English. Village life continued much as before, although now the peasants had to work the land and pay rent to new Norman masters instead of English ones.

Henry I wanted his daughter, Matilda, to succeed him but the barons didn't like the idea of a woman ruling England. They preferred her cousin, Stephen. Civil war broke out. Stephen won but Matilda got Normandy and it was agreed that, when Stephen died, her son, Henry II, would succeed to both Normandy and England. Henry II married Eleanor of Aquitaine in Eastern France and became king there too.

THE FIRST ENGLISH QUEEN?

But I'm the Queen!

During the war with Stephen, Matilda tried to arrange her own coronation at Westminster but an angry mob chased her from London so she was never crowned.

THE PLANTAGENTS

Henry II's family were known as Plantagenets after the sprig of broom (*planta genista*) his dad, the Duke of Anjou, wore in his hat! They spent most of their time quarrelling. All four of his sons declared war on Henry at one time or another, as did his wife, Eleanor.

Medieval kings saw themselves as warriors whose job was to protect their own land and win more. The barons' job was to help them do this. Everybody else was expected to work the fields and keep their rulers supplied with food and men to do their fighting.

THOMAS BECKET

Will no one rid me of this troublesome priest?

When Henry II's best friend Thomas, the Archbishop of Canterbury, took the Pope's side in an argument, some of Henry's knights murdered him in his cathedral. It's not clear if Henry gave the order.

I'd sell London to pay for my wars if I could.

I'd pay to keep him locked up.

Richard I only ever spent a few months in England which he saw mainly as a source of money to pay for his wars. He was very tall, whereas his brother John was quite short.

Henry was succeeded by Richard I, known as 'The Lionheart' because he loved fighting so much. When he was taken prisoner on his way back from the Crusades, the ransom to buy his freedom nearly bankrupted the country. Luckily for him his brother John's offer to pay more to keep him locked up was turned down.

When John became king after Richard's death, he managed to lose Normandy and Anjou to France. His barons got so fed up with his demands for money to pay for campaigns to win them back that they forced him to sign Magna Carta.

MAGNA CARTA 1215

Called Magna, meaning 'great', because it was very long, this document is hailed as the first time the King of England's power was limited by his subjects – but it only really protected the rights of the barons and bishops. Many rights didn't apply to most of the population – the poor farmworkers known as *villeins*. In any case, no sooner had he signed it than John tried to get out of his promises. The barons declared war on him which only ended with his death from illness the following year.

King John signed Magna Carta in a field at Runnymede beside the Thames

ROBIN HOOD

Although the stories we know about Robin were made up later, there were medieval pop songs about outlaws who stole from greedy kings and landowners.

THE CHURCH

The greatest power in medieval England, apart from the King, was the church which owned huge amounts of land, collected its own taxes and had great influence over the people. The church took its orders from the Pope in Rome which often caused a problem when kings, such as Henry II, fell out with him. Henry III rebuilt the magnificent Westminster Abbey we see today.

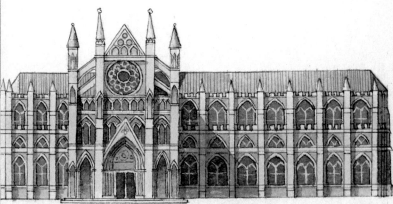

With so much land in France lost, John's grandson Edward I looked for conquests elsewhere. First he invaded Wales, built lots of castles and announced that his baby son would be the Prince of Wales. His conquest of Scotland was less successful. After his death, Robert Bruce smashed the English at Bannockburn (1314) and chased them out.

THE HUNDRED YEARS WAR 1337-1453

But the English kings couldn't forget the land in France they thought should still be theirs. For a hundred years, starting with Edward III, they led armies into France to try and win it back. When the king ran out of money to pay his soldiers, they often stayed on as bandits, stealing from the French.But in the end, after a fight led by Joan of Arc, the French chased them out and the only English bit left was the town of Calais.

AGINCOURT 1415

It is said Henry V's longbowmen made the 'V' for victory sign with their bowstring fingers after beating the French in the battle made famous by Shakespeare.

ROYAL MONEY–MAKING SCHEMES
Two great English institutions started as schemes to raise money to fight wars . . . .

THE ENGLISH LEGAL SYSTEM

Guilty! You owe the King some money.

Henry II realised that if his judges ran the courts they could also collect all the fines for the King to spend.

THE HOUSE OF COMMONS

I need £300,000 for my war.

In 1339, Edward III bypassed the barons by calling knights and rich merchants from towns and communities ('commons') to Westminster and asking them for money.

THE BLACK DEATH 1348

Despite frequent famine when harvests failed, the number of people in England may have reached 6 million by 1300. The plague called the Black Death probably killed as many as half of them.

THE PEASANTS REVOLT 1381

The Black Death killed so many people that there were not enough left to work the land. The rich landowners wanted the peasants who survived to work harder. The peasants demanded more money. Laws were passed making higher wages illegal . . .

. . . and to stop peasants dressing like rich people if they did get higher wages.

A priest called John Ball told the peasants they were just as good as lords and ladies.

When a new tax was levied which even peasants had to pay, thousands marched on London. 14–year–old King Richard II met them. Richard agreed to their demands but after a scuffle when their leader Wat Tyler was killed, he quickly went back on his word.

THE DUKE OF CLARENCE

drowned in wine

THE WARS OF THE ROSES
1455-1487

The Plantagenets kept up the quarrelling to the end. For thirty years two branches of the family, the Lancastrians and Yorkists, battled it out. Edward IV is said to have had his brother drowned in a barrel of wine and Richard III to have murdered his two nephews, one of whom was 13-year-old Edward V. In 1485 Henry Tudor, a distant Lancastrian cousin of the Yorkist Richard III, decided to challenge him for the crown.

THE PRINCES IN THE TOWER

never seen again

Henry Tudor defeated Richard III, who was killed at the battle of Bosworth in 1485.

It is said Richard's crown was found under a bush and placed on Henry's head.

In another story Richard's coffin was later emptied for use as a horse trough.

In 2012 bones thought to be Richard's were dug up in a Leicester carpark.

Henry Tudor, now Henry VII, combined the white rose of York and the red rose of Lancaster by marrying Elizabeth of York, older sister of the princes in the tower. He spent most of his reign making sure that all the taxes due to him were collected, and defending his throne. By the time he died the throne was secure and he had amassed a large fortune which he left to his son, Henry VIII.

ENGLAND AT THE END OF THE MIDDLE AGES

While the King and nobles quarrelled everybody else just got on with life. Many peasants now worked in small factories making woollen cloth. Wool, exported far and wide, had become England's most important source of wealth – so important that Edward III decided his Lord Chancellor should sit on a sack of it in the House of Lords. The Lord Chancellor still sits on a woolsack today.

VENETIAN DIPLOMAT 1497

The English think only England exists.

GERMAN TOURIST 1484

THE WOOLSACK

Lucky our ancestors brought those sheep over so I have a job.

Unmarried village women who spun wool were known as 'spinsters'.

THE ENGLISH LANGUAGE

Nearly all the Plantagenet kings spoke a type of French as their first language. Even Henry Tudor, who grew up in France, preferred to speak French. The language used by everybody towards the end of the Middle Ages was mostly a mixture of Anglo Saxon and Norman French, which became what we call English.

JOHN WYCLIFFE 1320–1384

GEOFFREY CHAUCER 1343–1400

WILLIAM CAXTON 1415–1492

helps to d in your tongue!

translated the Bible from Latin into English so everybody could read it.

wrote The Canterbury Tales in English we can just about understand today.

ran the first printing press in England and printed most of his books in English.

23

HENRY VIII

Henry inherited so much wealth from his dad that he was able to live in great splendour. He owned at least sixty palaces and is famous for having six wives. When his first wife, Catherine of Aragon, didn't seem able to have a son, he asked the Pope, as head of the Catholic Church, if he could have a divorce. The Pope refused, so Henry made himself head of the Church in England and gave himself a divorce.

After his 2nd wife, Anne, had a baby girl, Elizabeth, Henry had Anne beheaded for cheating on him.

His 3rd wife, Jane, eventually had a son, but she died soon after.

All I want is a son and heir!

Henry didn't even give his 5th wife time to have a baby before he had her beheaded for cheating.

He also beheaded two chief ministers who didn't get him what he wanted.

DIVORCED BEHEADED DIED DIVORCED BEHEADED SURVIVED

THE REFORMATION

Henry's split with the Catholic Church affected the lives of everybody in England. There were hundreds of monasteries, which owned huge amounts of land. Henry ordered the monks to be thrown out and the buildings pulled down. He took all their treasure and sold the land.

CATHOLIC V PROTESTANT

The Reformation led to centuries of conflict between Catholics and Protestants. Henry VIII's Protestant son, Edward, was King for only six years before he died aged fifteen. His older sister Mary, the daughter of Catherine of Aragon, followed him on the throne. Mary tried to return England to the Catholic Church. In 1558, the year she died, the French seized Calais, the very last English possession in France.

BLOODY MARY

I'm a Protestant because I protest against the power of the Pope.

Mary got this name for ordering Protestants to be burned at the stake.

QUEEN ELIZABETH I

Elizabeth's mum, Anne Boleyn, had been executed by her dad, Henry VIII. As queen, Elizabeth always tried to avoid quarrels. Her long and mostly peaceful reign is known as the 'Elizabethan Era', when the arts flourished and adventurers discovered new lands. Two conflicts she could not avoid were the plots to overthrow her in favour of Mary, Queen of Scots, and the Spanish Armada. She never married and had no children.

Elizabeth wore dresses covered in jewels and was nicknamed 'Gloriana' by her fans.

MARY QUEEN OF SCOTS

Elizabeth's cousin, Mary, also had a claim to the throne. Because she was Catholic, the Catholic supporters constantly plotted to make her Queen of England instead of the Protestant Elizabeth. Elizabeth reluctantly agreed to Mary's execution in 1587.

THE SPANISH ARMADA

In 1588 the Catholic King of Spain decided to rid himself of the Protestant Queen Elizabeth, and the English ships which plundered his galleons. But the English scattered his huge invasion fleet, the Armada, with fire ships and then a terrible storm destroyed much of his fleet.

During Elizabeth's reign English ships began to travel all over the globe in search of undiscovered lands. Virginia in America was named after Elizabeth, 'The Virgin Queen', but early attempts at colonisation failed. Jamestown, the first successful settlement, was named after her successor, James I, four years after her death.

SIR FRANCIS DRAKE 1540–1596

captured many Spanish treasure ships. He helped lead the English fleet against the Armada and led an expedition around the world in his ship Golden Hind.

SIR WALTER RALEIGH 1554–1618

never went to North America himself but organised expeditions to Virginia. He is often said to have introduced both the potato and tobacco to England.

WILLIAM SHAKESPEARE 1564–1616

Shakespeare is considered the greatest playwright who ever lived. He gave more words to the English language than any other writer and his plays are known around the world. Many had their first night at the Globe Theatre in London. Today a reconstruction stands near the site of the original building.

Elizabeth had no children. After her death Mary Queen of Scots' son, James, became King of England as well as Scotland, although the two countries kept separate parliaments. James upset both the Catholics and extreme Protestants, known as Puritans, by not taking sides with either of them.

THE GUNPOWDER PLOT 1605

A Catholic plot to blow James I up failed when Guy Fawkes was discovered with lots of gunpowder in the cellars of Parliament.

THE MAYFLOWER 1620

Puritan Pilgrims sailed across the Atlantic so they could worship freely in the land known as New England.

James's son, Charles I, believed he'd been created king by God, and so could do whatever he wanted. Parliament disagreed and refused to give him any money. The argument between them got so bad that it resulted in the English Civil War.

THE CIVIL WAR 1642–1651

The birds I came to catch have flown.

CAVALIERS
The King's side

ROUNDHEADS
Parliament's side

War broke out after Charles stormed into the House of Commons and tried to arrest some MPs. After several violent battles, Charles was captured and beheaded by the Roundheads. His son, Charles II, fled to France, hiding in an oak tree on the way.

THE COMMONWEALTH

At first the Roundheads decided they didn't want a king but Parliament couldn't agree how to run the country. Eventually they offered the crown to the Roundhead general, Oliver Cromwell. Although he refused it, he acted like a dictator, telling people what they could and couldn't do. To many, life under a king suddenly didn't seem so bad. When the quarrelling began again after Cromwell's death, Charles's son, Charles II, was invited back from exile.

OLIVER CROMWELL 1599–1658

Will you be king?

No, I'll just behave like one, OK?

Paint my portrait warts and all

Charles II's reign is notable for two terrible events – the Great Plague and the Great Fire of London – but it was also a time of exploration, trade and scientific discovery.

THE GREAT PLAGUE 1665

What's that, Doctor?

It keeps the plague out!

Hundreds of thousands died in the last big plague epidemic. People thought smoking or wearing masks would protect them.

THE GREAT FIRE 1666

The fire, which started in a baker's shop, burned almost the whole of the medieval City of London to the ground.

THE DUTCH INVASION 1688

Charles II's Catholic brother, James II, succeeded him. But James wasn't King for long. The Protestants encouraged his daughter, Mary, and her husband, the Dutch prince, William of Orange, to invade England. When William arrived with his troops crowds welcomed him into London.

Welcome

Goedemorgen

THE ROYAL SOCIETY

Granted a Royal charter in 1660, this famous institution has been at the forefront of worldwide progress in science and mathematics ever since. Early members include:

ROBERT BOYLE
physics and chemistry

ROBERT HOOKE
physics and chemistry

CHRISTOPHER WREN
architect of St Paul's

ISAAC NEWTON
maths and physics

The 18th century began with two important changes. In 1707 the Scottish and English Parliaments were joined together as the Parliament of Great Britain at Westminster. From now on English and Scottish history would often go hand in hand.

THE BANK OF ENGLAND 1694

·The government's bank started as another scheme to raise money for war, for ships to protect the new colonies and trade.

SIR ROBERT WALPOLE 1676–1745

Walpole is known as the first Prime Minister of Great Britain. The King gave him Number 10 Downing Street to live in.

'THE 15' and 'THE 45'

In 1715 and 1745, panic gripped England when James II's son and then his grandson led armies from Scotland to try and win back the crown. Both failed.

In 1701 the English Parliament had decided that only Protestants could succeed to the throne of England. So in 1714, after Mary's sister, Queen Anne, died childless, they passed over James II's Catholic son and instead invited a Protestant great-grandson of James I to be King. George I was a German prince. He spoke no English but that didn't matter. From now on the monarch would be a figurehead with no real power. Parliament was in charge.

THE TRIANGULAR TRADE

Many of the 18th century stately homes in England were built with the profits of the infamous 'Triangular Trade' which had begun during Elizabeth I's reign. Ships sailed from England to West Africa where they exchanged manufactured goods for African people. These people were crowded below decks in chains and sold as slaves to work on sugar plantations in the Caribbean colonies. Thousands died on the journey. The ships then returned to England loaded with valuable sugar. Sadly, the slave trade was not abolished until 1807.

As a result of the slave trade, thousands of African slaves, sailors and runaways found their way to England. Many English people today are descended from them.

TEA

Charles II's Portuguese wife, Catherine of Braganza, had made tea popular among posh English people. During the 18th century people of all classes began drinking it.

THE AMERICAN REVOLUTION

In 1776 the English colonists in America, fed up with being ruled and taxed from far-off England, declared their independence. The British government sent an army to try and stop them, but after seven years of war the Americans won and left the British Empire.

THE EAST INDIA COMPANY

The East India Company was also created in the time of Queen Elizabeth. By the 18th century its trade in cotton, tea and other goods from India and China made up half the world's trade. It even ruled large parts of India with its own private army!

TRANSPORTATION

In 1607 a London apprentice convicted of stealing was transported to the new colony of Virginia. Many more English convicts followed. After American independence, most were sent to Australia.

THE INDUSTRIAL REVOLUTION

This revolution, which began in England, changed the whole world. Wind and water had long been used to power mills. Now engineers found ways to improve them. Others experimented with steam engines. Coal was used for smelting iron and steel. Transport, chemical production, agriculture and mining all saw rapid change.

In 1710 Thomas Newcomen built the first steam engine as a pump for use in mines.

John Smeaton built new and better watermills, canals, bridges and lighthouses.

In 1769 Richard Arkwright invented a water-powered machine for spinning cotton.

Canals were dug between the ports and the new manufacturing centres of the Midlands and the North. But canals were soon eclipsed by steam railways. England sprouted railway lines everywhere well before most countries.

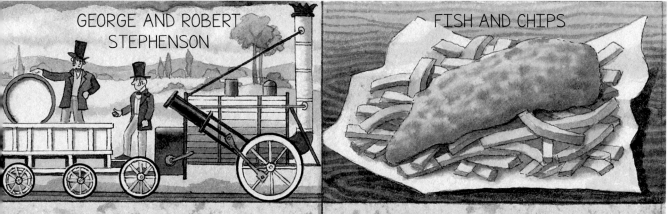

GEORGE AND ROBERT STEPHENSON

George and his son, Robert, built the first public steam railway in 1825. Their Rocket, now in London's Science Museum, set the design for steam locomotives for 150 years.

FISH AND CHIPS

Deep fried fish was introduced by Jewish refugees from Portugal. New railways rushed fresh fish to the industrial cities. Add chips and it was soon a national dish!

ISAMBARD KINGDOM BRUNEL 1806–1859
This giant of engineering built railways, dockyards, bridges, tunnels and astonishing new ships such as SS Great Britain, the first iron steam ship to cross the Atlantic.

NAPOLEON and THE THREAT OF INVASION

In 1793, soon after its Revolution, France declared war on Britain. When Napoleon took power in 1799 the threat of invasion got worse. You can still see the Martello towers built round the south coast of England to protect the terrified inhabitants.

People imagined all sorts of horrors, including scary looking French invasion machines.

TRAFALGAR 1805

Admiral Horatio Nelson was killed during his battle with the French and Spanish fleets, but victory ensured that Britain ruled the waves for the next century.

WATERLOO 1815

The Duke of Wellington's victory over Napoleon brought an end to war in Europe.

With the war over and their main rival defeated, British adventurers, merchants and politicians were able to concentrate on expanding the empire and getting rich.

THE VICTORIAN ERA 1837-1901

Queen Victoria's was the longest reign of any English monarch until Elizabeth II overtook her in 2015. The 19th century saw enormous growth and change. The population quadrupled despite millions emigrating to the colonies. As the number of people grew so did those who couldn't find jobs or homes. The Poor Law of 1834 created workhouses for them to live and work in. Life was very harsh for inmates so nobody wanted to be there unless they had no other choice.

CHARLES DICKENS 1812–1870

Please Sir, can I have some more?

The great English novelist campaigned against workhouses, like the one where Oliver Twist asked for more!

WILLIAM CUFFAY 1788–1870

You planned to make war on Queen Victoria.

Cuffay was a tailor whose dad had started life as a slave in the Caribbean. After he organised a large Chartist rally he was arrested and transported to Tasmania.

THE PEOPLE'S CHARTER 1838

In 1832 the Reform Act gave the vote to middle class men. Before that only the very richest people had been able to vote. The Chartists demanded a vote for every working man (although not for women). They held rallies attended by millions. The government banned them and arrested their leaders which led to the movement collapsing. It would not be until 1867 that some working men got the vote.

CHARLES DARWIN 1809–1882

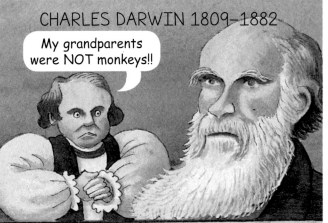

My grandparents were NOT monkeys!!

Darwin's 1859 book 'On the Origin of Species' changed the way we think about life by explaining how evolution works. Not everybody at the time was happy about it.

always give Dizzy primroses on his birthday.

BENJAMIN DISRAELI

WILLIAM GLADSTONE

Two Prime Ministers dominated Victoria's reign. Disraeli was her favourite.

The early 1900s saw the beginnings of the welfare state which we now take for granted. The government increased taxes to pay for old age pensions, support for the sick and unemployed, free school meals and better conditions in workhouses. Many of these reforms were driven by David Lloyd George, Chancellor and then Prime Minister during and after World War One.

DAVID LLOYD GEORGE 1863–1945

Four spectres haunt the poor...old age, accident, sickness and unemployment.

Born in Manchester to Welsh parents, he saw no reason why the rich should not pay tax towards taking care of the poor.

SUFFRAGETTES

In the early 1900s women campaigning for the vote chained themselves to railings, broke windows and even set off bombs. Hundreds were imprisoned and force fed with tubes when they went on hunger strike.

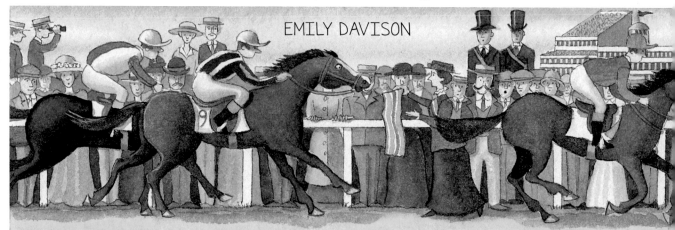

EMILY DAVISON

In 1913 Emily ran out on the course during the Epsom Derby to try and pin a suffragette banner on the King's horse. She was trampled and killed.

EDUCATION

Before the 19th century the few schools that existed were private or run by the church. Not much else was taught apart from learning to read the Bible. In 1833 Parliament voted to provide money to build more schools for the education of poor children. By the 1860s most children were getting an elementary education. This was made compulsory in 1888. In 1899 the school leaving age was raised to 12 and in 1918 to 14.

Ragged Schools had provided some free education for the poorest children. Their popularity in the 19th century proved the need for public funding of education.

WORLD WAR 1

In 1914, almost exactly a hundred years after the battle of Waterloo, English soldiers once more marched into Europe when Belgium asked for help after being invaded by Germany. World War One lasted for four years. There was fighting all over the world but most English soldiers fought in the trenches in Belgium and France.

Many men fought in the trenches alongside friends from their home town. In some battles, a whole generation of men from the same town were wiped out.

Millions of women worked in factories making ammunition or doing the jobs of the men who'd left to fight. They proved themselves the equal of men.

POPPY DAY

Poppies, like the ones which grew on the battlefields, are still worn to mark 11th November, the day the war ended in 1918.

Nearly every family lost somebody in the war. You can find war memorials in almost every town and village of England. As if that wasn't bad enough, a flu epidemic killed another quarter of a million people in 1918-19.

Many changes followed the war. Working men who had fought in the trenches knew they were just as good as upper class officers. Women, who had done men's jobs, didn't want to go back to being servants. In 1918 all men over 21 and women over 30 got the vote. As a result, in 1924 the first Labour Government was elected.

Young middle class women, known as flappers, wore short hair and dresses and danced to jazz.

The BBC's first radio broadcast was in 1922. Soon most households had a radio.

THE GREAT DEPRESSION

Between 1929-1933, following a worldwide economic crisis, Britain's trade fell by half. Millions lost their jobs. Many were left penniless. In 1931 the government brought in a system which ensured that all those who were unemployed received some money. After 1933 things gradually began to improve.

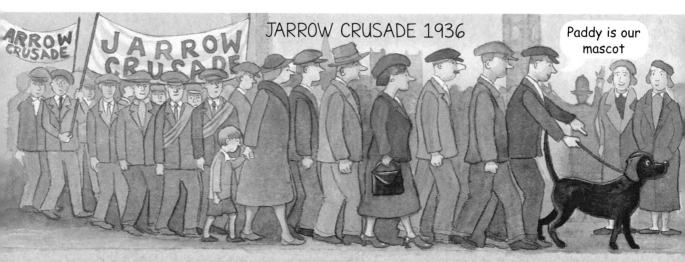

When the depression forced a shipyard in Jarrow on Tyneside to close, 200 jobless people marched to London to ask for help. The Prime Minister refused to meet them.

WORLD WAR 2

In 1939 war broke out again. Germany invaded France and England once more faced the threat of invasion.

In 1940 Spitfire and Hurricane airplanes defeated the Germans over southern England during the Battle of Britain, making the country safer from invasion.

THE BLITZ 1940–1941

London and other large cities faced night after night of bombing which killed many and destroyed whole streets.

BLITZ KIDS

Nearly a million children were evacuated from cities to live with families in the country, away from the fear of bombing.

THE HOME GUARD

It's from the museum!

This was my grandad's!

Older men and men unfit for the regular army joined 'Dad's Army' to defend England in case of invasion. To begin with they had to improvise weapons.

WINSTON CHURCHILL 1874–1965

We'll defend our island whatever the cost.

BBC

The famous wartime PM cheered people up with his speeches and the one-piece 'siren suits' he wore when the air raid sirens got him out of bed in the middle of the night.

By the time Germany was defeated, bombing had destroyed half a million homes.

After the war nobody wanted a return to the hardship and poverty of the Victorian era and the Great Depression. Millions of new houses had to be built to replace slums and bomb damage. In 1948 the National Health Service was created to provide free healthcare for all. Today the NHS in England employs over a million people.

People from all over the world were welcomed to help rebuild industry and services. In 1948 the first of England's Afro-Caribbean community sailed from Jamaica on a ship, called the *Empire Windrush*. Over the following years many more came from India, Pakistan, China, Africa and other parts of Britain's former Empire.

EMPIRE WINDRUSH
LONDON

QUEEN ELIZABETH II

After her father's death, 25–year–old Elizabeth was crowned in 1953. Many predicted a new Elizabethan age. She is the longest reigning English monarch.

In the years after the war most of Britain's overseas colonies became independent. More and more the UK turned towards Europe and in 1973 joined what is now called the European Union. Since then many people from other European countries have made England their home, while many English people have chosen to live and work in Europe.

TOP 20th CENTURY TECHNOLOGY

During and after the war, England was home to a number of technological developments which have changed travel, medicine, agriculture, industry and how we process information, in ways our ancestors could never have imagined.

THE JET ENGINE

Sir Frank Whittle invented the turbo jet before the war. This led in 1952 to the Comet, the very first jet airliner, and the birth of mass air travel.

THE COMPUTER

In 1936 Alan Turing invented the Turing Machine, leading to the development of computers after the war, without which modern life would grind to a halt.

THE DOUBLE HELIX

In 1953 Watson, Crick and Franklin identified the double helix shape of DNA, transforming our understanding of genetics and how life and disease work.

THE WORLD WIDE WEB

English computer scientist, Sir Tim Berners Lee, invented the Web in 1981. Today we rely on its interlinked pages for more and more of our information.

Many sports played around the world today, such as soccer, cricket, rugby, tennis, squash and snooker were first played or had their rules drawn up in England. In 2012 London hosted the Olympics for the third time, the only world city to have done so more than twice.

Mo Farah, who was born in Somalia, and Jessica Ennis from Sheffield were two English 2012 Olympic champions.

In 2010 Russian born scientists, Sir Andre Geim and Sir Konstantin Novoselov working in Manchester found how to make graphene, the thinnest, lightest, strongest material ever. One day it may be used to build an elevator into space!

CHICKEN TIKKA MASALA

Thought to have originated in England when an Indian chef added Masala sauce to Chicken Tikka. In 2001 the Foreign Secretary declared this a national dish.

THE ENGLISH LANGUAGE IN THE 21st CENTURY

Although English is not as widely spoken as Mandarin Chinese or Spanish it is the language most often used when people with different native languages speak to each other. It is also the language most often used in books, films, television, the internet and in science. All from a small country on a small island on the edge of Europe.

The Story of England

12,000 BC   Modern humans arrive in England

6,000 BC   Surrounding ice has melted leaving Britain as an island

3,000 - 2,000 BC   Stonehenge built

43 AD   Julius Caesar and his Roman legions invade England

128 AD   Hadrian's Wall completed

600 AD   Anglo Saxons rule over most of England

870 AD   Vikings settle in eastern England

1066 AD   Battle of Hastings

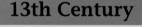

13th Century

1215   Magna Carta signed by King John

14th Century

1314   Robert the Bruce defeats English forces at Bannockburn

1337   Hundred Years War begins

1348   The Black Death kills millions

1381   Wat Tyler leads the Peasants' Revolt

15th Century

1437   Hundred Years War ends

1455   War of the Roses begin

1476   William Caxton introduces the first printing press to England

1485   Henry Tudor defeats Richard III to become King Henry VII

1487   War of the Roses end

16th Century

1509   Henry VII dies and his son, Henry VIII, becomes King

1559   Elizabeth I becomes Queen

1587   Mary Queen of Scots executed

1588   The Spanish Armada defeats the King of Spain's forces

1594   Shakespeare's company performs *Romeo and Juliet* for the first time

17th Century

1603   Queen Elizabeth I dies and Mary Queen of Scots' son, James, becomes King of England and Scotland

1605   The Gunpowder Plot is discovered

1620   The Mayflower sets sail across the Atlantic, taking Puritan Pilgrims to New England

1625   James I dies and his second son, Charles I, becomes King

1642   The English Civil War begins between Parliament's Roundheads and the King's Cavaliers. Charles I is executed in 1649 but the war continues until 1651

1653   Oliver Cromwell becomes Lord Protector

1665   The Great Plague kills thousands

1666   The Great Fire of London destroys much of the old City

1694   The Bank of England established

18th Century

1707   Scottish and English parliaments join together to form the Parliament of Great Britain

1710   Thomas Newcomen creates the first industrial steam engine

1714   German-born George I becomes King

1721   Sir Robert Walpole becomes first Prime Minister

1776   The American Revolution begins. The fighting will lasts for seven years until English forces are defeated and America gains its independence

1793   France declares war on England

19th Century

1805   Battle of Trafalgar - Admiral Nelson is killed

1815   English forces defeat the French at Waterloo

1825   George and Robert Stephenson build the first public steam railway

1837   Queen Victoria's sixty-four year reign begins

1859   Charles Darwin's *On the Origin of Species* published

1888   Elementary education becomes compulsory

20th Century

1901 Queen Victoria dies, Edward VII becomes King

1910 Edward's oldest son, George, becomes King George V

1914 First World War begins

1918 First World War ends, and men over 21 and women over 30 are given the vote

1929 Great Depression begins

1933 Great Depression ends

1936 Alan Turing builds the Turing Machine

1936 Edward VIII becomes King but abdicates after 325 days, passing the crown to his brother, George VI

1939 Second World War begins

1945 Second World War ends

1948 NHS created

1948 First of England's Afro-Caribbean community arrive from Jamaica

1953 Elizabeth II crowned

1953 The shape of DNA identified by scientists in London and Cambridge

1981 Tim Berners Lee invents the World Wide Web

21st Century

2012 England hosts the Olympics for the third time

2015 Queen Elizabeth II becomes England's longest reigning monarch

ENGLAND
AFTER
1485

JOHN CABOT
in 1497 he was probably the first European to set foot in North America since the Vikings. Although an Italian, real name Giovanni Caboto, Henry VII had paid for the trip and claimed Newfoundland for England.

JOHN BULL
the typical English country gentleman who first appeared in a book in 1712, soon caught on with other writers and artists. Often shown eating roast beef.

PUNCH & JUDY
Italian puppeteers brought Mr Punch to England in the 17th century. He soon became a national institution.

BOSCOBEL
Charles II's oak tree

BRISTOL

SS GREAT BRITAIN

MAYFLOWER
set sail for America from Plymouth in 1620

where Drake played bowls before the Armada

where the Dutch Invasion landed in 1688

Second World War pillbox

WHEAL VOR MINE
Newcomen engine

TORBAY

PLYMOUTH

EDDYSTONE ROCK – Smeaton's Lighthouse

STOCKTON & DARLINGTON RAILWAY 1825

MARSTON MOOR 1644
the biggest battle of the Civil War

JARROW
where the crusade set out from

NORTH SEA

THE ARMADA
blown north by storms

CROMFORD
Arkright's first watermill

FOTHERINGHAY CASTLE
where Mary Queen of Scots was executed

Martello Tower

DERBY
where Bonnie Prince Charlie turned back after invading England in 1745

BLETCHLEY PARK

CAMBRIDGE

ST PAUL'S CATHEDRAL

TILBURY
where Elizabeth I made her Armada speech and the Empire Windrush arrived

HAMPTON COURT
Henry VIII's palace

GREENWICH

GLOBE THEATRE

DOWNE
Charles Darwin's house

BATTLE OF BRITAIN

DEAL CASTLE
built by Henry VIII

EPSOM DERBY

Les Rosbifs!

BARBARY PIRATES
between 1600–1800 North African pirates raided the coast taking thousands of English people as slaves